It Ain't Easy but It's Worth It:

Ten Keys to Positive Changes that Last

Sohlea Rico

Sohlea Rico

208-2202 Lambert Dr.

Courtenay, BC, Canada V9N 1Z8

info@guidingpositivechange.com

www.guidingpositivechange.com

Limits of Liability and Disclaimer of Warranty

Dedication

To Nina and Marvin Haave
My loving and always supportive parents

Do you want to make lasting positive change in your life?

- Sign up for the free monthly *Guiding Positive Change Newsletter* at www.guidingpositivechange.com and check out blog articles of interest

- Try the personal coaching, healing packages, workshops and classes of Sohlea Rico of Guiding Positive Change

- You can Skype, use Google Hangouts, or phone from anywhere in the world or come in person to Courtenay, BC, Canada

- Experience rapid and lasting transformation in thinking, behaviors, feelings and physical wellbeing

- The approach is tailored to your unique needs and personality

- Get one on one attention from a relaxed and highly skilled practitioner

- I specialize in working with middle-aged women and my work is suitable for other adults

- Do you wonder if working with *Guiding Positive Change* will be a good fit for you? Contact Sohlea Rico at info@guidingpositivechange.com to arrange a *free fifteen minute consultation* by Skype or phone.

Acknowledgements

My heartfelt thanks go out to all the teachers who have given me guidance and support in my life's journey.

Thanks to all my clients and friends over the years who have taught me so much about the amazing strength and resilience of people and their capacity to heal and grow.

Kudos to Linda Graceffo for the beautiful cover design and her fantastic service (www.selfpublishingresources.ca) and to Donna Kozik for teaching me how to write a book and bring my writing alive (www.writewithdonna.com).

I'm grateful to my partner Arlene for her ongoing challenge, encouragement and editing skills and to other friends for inspiration and editing assistance.

About the Author

I'm guessing you might be feeling a little stuck in old ways of thinking and being that you can't seem to get past. You want to relax, be at peace with yourself and offer your gifts to the world. You don't know exactly what's holding you back or how to change but you are ready and willing. You just need a little help.

I'm Sohlea Rico founder of *Guiding Positive Change*. I blend ancient spiritual wisdom with modern scientific approaches to provide guidance and tools to help people like you find your unique strengths and create what you want in life. I've been diving deeply into personal and spiritual development and health and healing since 1988. I'm passionate about helping people make positive change as easily as possible.

What I do is guide my clients to remember what they really want, to own their internal strengths, to find the unconscious roots of their problems and then let that stuck stuff go as quickly and easily as possible so they can get on with a happier and more meaningful life. I'm also adept at helping people heal issues of the body and working with energy. For more details about me and how I work, check out my website www.gudingpositivechange.com.

I have a Masters Degree in Transformative Leadership, am a registered physical therapist, a Neuro Linguistic Programming (NLP) practitioner, a Matrix Energetics practitioner and a channel. I've worked in management, leadership and community development, and studied and taught ancient yogic philosophies. I have deep experience in mind/body healing and spiritual practice. One of my big life adventures was initiating the Creekside Commons cohousing community on Vancouver Island, Canada where I now live with my life-partner Arlene.

The delights in my life include being active in nature, connecting with people, and playing in the kitchen cooking and brewing up healthy foods. If I seem familiar but you can't put a name to my face, I changed my name from Sharon Haave to Sohlea Rico (first name pronounced Solay) on Jan 1, 2014.

Many of my clients are middle-aged women but you'll find that this book is written for anyone who is keen on making positive personal change. So check it out and see what you find! Browse through this book in whatever way you wish. You can discover—or refresh in your mind—the *10 Keys* to making lasting personal change. You are in charge of your life so you'll find your own unique ways to make the changes you want in your life and the world.

To sign up for my free monthly newsletter, read more of my articles, connect about the possibility of working together, ask a question or give me feedback, head to www.guidingpositivechange.com

I look forward to connecting with you!

Sohlea

Contents

Introducing the Keys to Positive Change

If you've picked up this book, I'm guessing you want to make some positive changes in your life. Creating lasting change isn't always easy. It takes courage and persistence to break down old ways of thinking and acting, most of which have been with you for many years. Still, there are ways to make this path of change happen more smoothly— sometimes with amazing grace and ease!

I've explored many different things on my own journey of making positive change: ancient yoga, Neuro Linguistic Programming, mind-body connections, health and healing, and personal and spiritual development in many forms. This book is a compilation of TEN KEY things I have learned along the way about creating positive personal change. As well as my own thoughts and questions in each chapter, you will find quotes from inspiring women to further stimulate your process.

The science of the brain has been a leading-edge topic over the last couple of decades. Through technologies like brain scanners and computers, scientists have learned more about the brain in the last while than in all the centuries of recorded knowledge before that. These discoveries are reinforcing what ancient traditions have known intuitively for thousands of years—that changing the brain, along with our thinking and behavior is possible through persistence and the application of central principles.

It's exciting to know that you are not stuck with what has been created in the past. It *is* possible to change for the better, and it may not be as hard as you think. The journey to positive change is interesting, engaging and rewarding. You will move past thinking and behaviors that limit you, even the fears that hold you back, while growing into the person you want to be and claiming the life you want to live.

You will be using your whole mind, both its logic and intuition, to gather what you need from this book. The chapters are designed to build on one another so reading or scanning through the chapters in the order they are presented will provide some context. That being said, after you read the table of contents, you can also trust your instincts on where to go next, what to quickly scan and what to read in depth.

There's no right or wrong way to collect your tools for change, so go ahead and dive into the subjects that engage you. You can make your exploration personal by reflecting on your life experience and considering how each of these *KEYS* will apply to your situation.

I know that you can make the changes you desire and because of that, I am here cheering you on! By staying open and asking for it, you will find all the guidance and support you need along the way. Dive in and have fun!

Sohlea

The First Key:
Open to Your Curiosity

"I think at a child's birth, if a mother could ask a fairy godmother to endow it with the most useful gift, that gift would be curiosity." Eleanor Roosevelt

Think back to the kind of curiosity you had when you were a little kid. You wanted to know about everything and how things were connected. People all start out with the infinite curiosity of a fresh and open beginner's mind. Playful and spontaneous curiosity is still inside you. Bringing it forward is the *FIRST KEY* in your journey towards positive change.

Since it's so important, why don't people naturally use this curiosity about life in adulthood? That's because it has been socialized out of you. Curious adults who want to know what's really going on are a risk to the status quo—both inside and out. When I started to explore what was in my unconscious mind and who I was under the surface, I came up against my own resistance and fear. I had dreams where I could only dive so far into water before panic caused me to swim back up to the surface. These dreams brought forward the fear of what I might discover deep within: that the emotions and feelings I had bottled up and tried so hard to control would suddenly explode in a way I wouldn't be able to handle. With the help of curiosity, I learned to dive a little more deeply each time. I've discovered that most fear and apparent dangers are products of my imagination. Instead of going there, I cultivated curiosity about who I am and what makes me tick.

I call the part of myself that helps me get interested in, rather than afraid of, what I might find inside me, "the curious adventurer". This personality aspect has become a good friend and companion on my journey of self-discovery. My "curious adventurer" is a cross between Harrison Ford in the *Raiders of the Lost Ark* movie (I know, I'm dating myself!), slashing through the thick jungle and swinging across wild rivers on a vine, and a quiet scientist looking with keen interest through a magnifying glass, excited and captivated by what is there. I call on this inner quality when doubt and fear threaten my capacity to open to what my unconscious mind presents, although that is rarely an issue now.

If you look within, you too will discover aspects that you can call on when the going gets scary. Continuing on a journey of positive change does require courage and conviction to overcome the habits and beliefs that keep you stuck. Learning about yourself activates an endless source of interest in what you will find. When you are curious, everything becomes an opportunity to gather more information and to allow something new to emerge. "I wonder what it would be like if…" or "That's interesting", said in times of uncertainty and confusion, can frame what's happening in a way that brings in relaxation and opens new possibilities. Bringing forward an "interested witness" (another personality aspect) not attached to any specific outcome allows your journey to become an adventure. While you might still have some fear, you will be able to take a big breath and step into the unknown, ready to explore. You can't know what will happen or where it might lead— and that doesn't really matter. What does matter is that willingness to explore.

Moving Past Fear

Why is it so difficult to conquer fears from the past? Fear triggers an innate physiological response. You know the feeling—your breathing stops then gets rapid and short. All of your senses are on high alert. The front of your body protectively contracts, your jaw clenches and you can no longer think rationally. This is called the "fight, flight or freeze response". Your body prepares for possible danger by getting ready to put up a fight, run for the hills, or freeze in the attempt to become invisible. As a reflex, it is involuntary and very fast, so it will happen whether you want it to or not.

Human physiology hasn't changed much since people first walked the earth and lived in caves, but there are many more stimuli in modern life that trigger this self-protective response. Humans are hard wired for survival. Fear is an appropriate and useful reaction when you are in actual physical danger, because it helps you move quickly out of potentially harmful situations to save your skin. However, when you are in that state of fear you are poorly equipped to make decisions. Your resources are focused on primitive areas of your brain and on your muscles, away from the frontal cortex where you figure things out and make decisions.

Not much learning can happen in this state of fear, which is meant to keep people in safe old patterns and ways of thinking. Fear tells you to stick to the ways of the tribal unit and to avoid venturing into the unknown. That strategy was useful in an era when wandering away from the tribe or into the cave of a wild animal could mean death or injury. Have you ever considered that your ancestors were people who obeyed fear and kept themselves safe and alive? People who stepped too far out of the box died (and didn't go on to reproduce offspring)! In this modern world, however, that kind of fear that is hard wired into humans stops you from breaking out of the status quo and finding your way to the life you want to live. It takes courage and awareness to step beyond fear and find out what's possible.

Most fears are not actually warranted in the modern world and they limit you from taking positive action toward what you want. Inappropriate fears are those that come from imagination and are based in future expectations. If you imagine that something will happen, your body will react as if what you imagine is real. The unconscious mind isn't able to differentiate between the real and the imagined, so the imagined fear message from your conscious mind is understood by your unconscious mind as a fact and you soon find yourself experiencing all the bodily and emotional responses associated with fear. You find yourself protecting and shutting down.

Besides genetically, how else do these habits of inappropriate fear get started? Why do we have them at all if they don't serve us positively? Many unconscious programs of inappropriate or unwarranted fear begin when people are young (and they can start at any time of life through trauma). With any kind of trauma, no matter how big or small, children find ways to create safety, to win the care of parents and survive. These survival mechanisms were created for good reason; they did serve a purpose when you were young. After all, you're still here aren't you? However, the same fears are often inappropriate later in life. They become limitations when they turn on automatically every time you face an experience like the one that set it up in childhood. For example, fear of the dark may have brought the attention and protection of parents when you were a child but would limit you now as an adult.

Fears are also learned behaviors. If your mother was afraid of authority figures, you may also carry it as a limiting fear learned from her as a child. There are cultural fears shared by whole groups, such as the North American fear of losing independence, which can paradoxically lead to isolation and loneliness. Fear of failure is also common in our competitive Western society. The message from our culture is that failure is to be avoided at all costs. Should it happen, it is to be covered up. We're all aware of the cover-ups of politicians, professionals, and leaders who have made mistakes they aren't willing to admit. In the dominant culture, "winners" are rewarded and "losers" are punished and downgraded.

Why is it hard to grow out of these limiting behaviors that are based in fear? One reason is that you get biochemical rewards for sticking to old patterns, whether they now serve you or not. The feel-good chemical dopamine is released when you behave in ways that adhere to the rules or follow what you believe to be true. If you think you must be perfect or at least not make mistakes, you will get a feel-good rush of endorphins by behaving in acceptable ways. You may even experience the release of feel-bad chemicals when you fail to follow old patterns or try something new, leaving you feeling anxious or worse.

It *is* hard to install new patterns of thinking when conforming to the certainty of old beliefs is both pleasurable and addictive. You will need courage and conviction to go without the positive chemical hit that comes with the certainty of the status quo.

The paradox of this human preference for known successes and a tenacious avoidance of failure is that most learning can only happen through trial and error. When you do try new things, the resulting feedback teaches you to make different, more refined choices in future trials. You keep getting better at what you are practicing, you are able to relax and you move incrementally towards what you want. Since we only learn well when relaxed and since fear of punishment or ostracism for failing creates tension, people most easily go into survival mode—a poor state for learning. Cultivating curiosity, along with the courage and willingness to try things out *in spite of* your fear of the unknown or of failure will allow you to learn and grow.

Choice

The journey of self discovery and making positive change is a constantly renewing process of making choices, taking action, getting feedback, readjusting, taking another action and repeating the cycle over and over again. Remember that there is no perfect choice. Make the best choice you can think of at the time and then try it out. Be open to the guidance and feedback that come as a result of your action, then adjust accordingly and take another step. By tolerating small failures as a potentially useful and necessary stage of learning, failure becomes acceptable.

I think of the choices in life like being in a hallway with doors on either side. You exit through one door, leaving behind something you are finished with (or that's finished with you!). You may find yourself standing in a long hallway looking across at any number of doors. Perhaps one of them will open and you can simply walk through to the next thing in your life. Sometimes you have to try many different doors to find one that opens. Sometimes no door opens when you first try them. Sometimes going into something new is easy; sometimes it's really hard. When things get uncomfortable and feel foreign, you may go through a period of regret thinking you went through the wrong door or shouldn't have walked out of the old one in the first place. It can take time to settle into something new and see that what you left behind no longer fit and what you have walked into is perfect for your learning and growth.

If it seems like you have been waiting in the hallway for a long time and nothing is happening I've noticed that it doesn't work to put your shoulder to a door and slam hard to force it open like they do in police shows. You'll probably just hurt yourself that way, or at the very least, damage a perfectly good door. If you knock on the all the doors you see, if you try all the knobs and none of them opens, you might have to stand in the hallway for a while until one does open. Sometimes the lights get turned off and life can seem pretty dark and uncertain—hopefully there's a chair for you to wait in!

It takes trust to stay in the hallway of the unknown and wait. I've certainly been there. It's a challenge not to run back through an old familiar door to the safety of what is already known. It's not easy to wait for something beyond what you can conceive of or control. There may be possibilities way beyond what you can imagine that will be behind the door that opens. As hard as it can be to sit in the unknown and perhaps in the darkness, the waiting itself is part of the journey. You can think of it as a time of ripening, or a time of "being" to balance the "doing". Remember that any fearful scenarios that arise about the future are created by your imagination. They haven't yet and aren't likely to happen, so settle in, get a bowl of popcorn and try being patient. The right door for your next steps *will* open when you are ready and the time is right.

Through my experience as a therapist and teacher, I've listened to many stories about people's lives. What I've learned through that listening is that people are basically made of the same stuff. Everyone has bad things happen to them, some very tragic and hard. Everyone has done things that they regret. You may sometimes wish you had made different choices or wonder what your life would have been like if you had. You may not always deal well with your emotions. Know that you are not alone in the painful things of life (or the joyful ones for that matter). There is nothing that you have experienced that someone else hasn't also. Keeping secrets in shame tends to makes things worse. Being open and sharing what you are experiencing and feeling helps to release the fear and tension of thinking you are the only one with this problem.

People all have tough stuff to go through and everyone makes mistakes. It's what you do with what happens in your life that counts. Did you learn from it? Have you become a different person because of it? Are you making different choices because of the wisdom you've gained? If you have, then acknowledge the victories and what it takes to make something sweet out of something that once seemed sour. If you haven't, you still have the opportunity. Find and cultivate the inner resources you need to take risks and to find out who you really are. What makes you tick and what do you want from this precious lifetime? Learn to be resilient about failure, to not take it personally but to look at it as useful guidance.

Know that when you seek fulfillment and a life of purpose there will always be some fear. Decide that creating what you want in your life and taking the steps to get you there are worth the effort. Find the *KEY* to your own curious adventurer to help you along the way. Finally, be patient. Sometimes you might have to wait a bit.

First Key: Things to Try

1. Notice what gets you curious, what you are interested in and what you like to learn about. Write about it. Follow your "learning edge"—the things that capture your attention. They'll take you to your purpose and passions.

2. Notice which of your senses: sight, hearing, touch, taste, or smell, come forward when you are interested in something or learning something new. They are your easiest doorways to curiosity and learning. Pay attention to the wisdom of your body: What does your heart say? What are you feeling in your gut? Listen to the wisdom of your body.

3. Think about how you learn. Do you prefer to see someone doing something, to read about it, to try it out for yourself? How many times do you need to see it or try it to be convinced it is of value for you? When you want to learn something, including learning about yourself, you can use this information to find the way that's right for you.

The Second Key:
Know That Anything is Possible

"When nothing is sure, everything is possible." Margaret Drabble

What do you think is possible? Have you noticed that what you expect to have happen *is* what usually happens? According to quantum physics, there are infinite numbers of possibilities available in the universe at any given time and what you focus on and expect is what tends to happen. The quantum world is waiting for you to make a decision about what you expect so it knows how to behave. The information from your thoughts, emotions, beliefs and intentions is constantly informing the quantum reality within and around you and creating what you think of as your reality. Sometimes what's happening suits you just fine and other times, not so much. Perhaps you would prefer something else to be happening in terms of what you are experiencing. What if you could access many other possible outcomes and change what you are experiencing?

Trying to create new possibilities by using just your rational left-brain or conscious mind doesn't tend to work. The conscious mind is a serial (and serious!) processor that thinks in sequences of cause and effect, such as when this happens, this will happen next and so on. It doesn't understand things like universal possibility. The rational mind is really useful when you want to figure things out, such as how to put together kit furniture or balance your checkbook or follow a recipe. But when you focus on what's not working and on what's still the same, your unconscious mind is directed to pay attention only to possibilities you already know. When you focus on a possibility that has already materialized, that possibility trumps anything new and grows stronger—there's no room for anything else.

Accessing infinite possibility actually has more to do with your heart and its creativity. The heart is a complex, self-organized information-processing center with its own functional brain that communicates with the brain in the head. The magnetic field of the heart is 60 times larger than that of the brain and radiates out five to ten feet away from you. Your heart has a profound influence on most body systems, your perceptions and responses to the world, your intelligence and awareness and ultimately determines the quality of your life.

There are simple ways of inviting new possibilities into your body, mind and life. Start with taking your awareness to your heart center in the middle of your chest. Some people call this "dropping into the heart". People's awareness is often focused on thinking with the brain, but your awareness can be located anywhere inside or outside of your body. Notice where your awareness is and consciously bring it into your heart center (check the "Things to Try" section at the end of the chapter for more details).

Once you are in your heart, set an intention for what you want to experience a shift in. It's useful to phrase what you want in the positive. For example, "I'd like to have a strong comfortable shoulder" (*not* "I don't want a weak uncomfortable shoulder"), or "I want a supportive and harmonious relationship with my sister", or "I wish to have this upcoming meeting go smoothly with an outcome that supports everyone".

The next step is to let go of thinking about what you want. Let go of expectations of what may or may not happen while being curious about what might be possible or what might show up. Watch for anything that changes in your perception, thinking, or physical sensations and emotions.

Bringing your awareness to your heart in this way allows the vast capacities of the unconscious mind to connect with universal or infinite possibility. When that happens, something new can manifest. If you want something different to happen, lighten up, experiment and become playful. Bring forward your childlike curiosity and wonder and play with the possibilities of the universe. (For more about the heart field, the *fifth KEY* goes into more detail.)

In creating positive change it's important to pay attention to what's different rather than what's the same. Training yourself to notice what is different, positive, beautiful, happy, and supportive of the best in you takes practice. It establishes new brain patterns that will help you create what you want in your life. Since the human brain is wired for survival, part of that strategy is to pay attention to what's the same as things you've experienced in the past—things that would best be avoided or sought out. Scanning for potential dangers and noticing and remembering negative experiences are part of the human survival imperative, as is clinging to what feels safe. It takes awareness and persistent effort to shift out of noticing what's *not* resourceful for you and changing to noticing what *is* useful or what might be possible.

Certainty and Uncertainty

When you take your awareness into the creative heart field and allow space for other possibilities to come forward, you move from the certainty of what's known into the unknown. It's an uncomfortable place for the conscious mind—like the discomfort of waiting in the hallway from the *first KEY*. It can seem dark, vulnerable, and confusing when you don't know what's happening and you can't control it.

Do you notice that when you feel uncertain, you want to get back to what is familiar as quickly as you can? That's because focusing on what's the same brings certainty. You know what to expect and you find safety and comfort in that familiar place, even if it's not serving you well. Unfortunately, you may be eliminating possibilities that could allow something different, new and useful to emerge. The more you try to create certainty and order, the more elusive it can be.

Notice when and where you have a desire or tendency to make a quick fix in order to return to certainty. When you feel uncertain about something, can you hang out there for a while? Can you bring forward curiosity and courage and invite something new into your world?

Duality and Projection: Thinking in Black and White

Western culture is set up in terms of opposites such as black and white, good and bad, right and wrong, up and down. Just as in the preference for certainty over uncertainty and order over chaos, people learn to prefer one side of a duality over the other. What's ironic is that by focusing on one side of a duality, such as good or up or right, you actually notice and strengthen the other side too—bad, down, wrong. One can't exist without the other, so as you focus on the good, you naturally keep an eye out for what might be bad.

What happens when someone disagrees with your strong beliefs? Do you feel self-righteous? Do you try to convince them or your rightness and their wrongness? Do you find yourself justifying your position? People hold strong beliefs based on the dualities of their culture: what's right and wrong or good and bad. A belief is a creation of the mind, an opinion. People hold many differing opinions about the same things—what I think of as wrong you may think of as right. It's hard to change patterns and behaviors based on a belief because it feels good to think you are right, no matter what the belief. As I mentioned in the *first KEY*, each time you think in a way that adheres to your current beliefs, the "feel-good" chemical, dopamine, is released in your body and you get a biochemical reward for your thinking. Beliefs are not inherently right or wrong, they are just beliefs, but both parties feel biochemically good when sticking to their side in a dispute about what they think is right and true.

No wonder there is so much disagreement and conflict in the world! It feels good, at least in the moment, to prefer one side of a duality and hold to the accompanying beliefs. It takes a lot of courage to deny a delicious biochemical hit of certainty and rightness, to see what is really happening and to step out of the familiar and known to allow something else to come forward. Being in the unknown may not feel as good as being right, but being curious and interested in whatever might be happening without preference allows other possibilities to come forward.

Which brings me to another difficulty in opening to possibility: What happens when you can't acknowledge one side of a duality as being within yourself? Strange as it may seem, you will usually see it in and project it onto another person or group until you are willing and able to see it in yourself.

Projection can happen both with what you think is unacceptable and also with what you think is acceptable. The other person or group is seen as bad, wrong, lazy, and arrogant or perhaps even wise and wonderful (or whatever parts you aren't willing to own in yourself). Groups project when they blame or applaud another group for something they are unable to acknowledge or appreciate in their community. Projection results in conflict and suffering both in individuals and in the world and limits your growth.

When someone else is doing something you don't like, try looking inside—it probably applies to you in some way as well. The same holds true for all the qualities you see in others that you admire. When you can accept your own wholeness—both the light and dark aspects of a duality, you're less likely to judge or become jealous and are more likely to celebrate the differences that make up this interesting world. It allows for an integral wholeness in life that is real.

When a disowned part of you has been pushed out of awareness, it may become a saboteur, leading to inappropriate and unexpected thinking and behaviors. For example, anger that is easily seen in others but not allowed to come forward consciously in oneself may be expressed instead as overblown, self-righteous reactions which result in suffering both for you and others. Acknowledging anger or any other disowned emotion can allow it to mature and become a potentially useful part of you. Anger, for instance, can be a mobilizing force that motivates people to make positive change.

When positive qualities are disowned but seen in others instead of yourself, those parts also aren't available to you. What you admire in others is part of you or you wouldn't even recognize it. Humans are wired to notice what's not working and as part of that, people tend to know and own their weaknesses much more their strengths. Focusing on your weaknesses just makes them stronger. It's helpful to make a list of your strengths and inner resources and become comfortable and familiar with them. Look for them in your daily actions and make them friends and allies in your life. They are there to help you. Focus on using your strengths and improving them rather than strengthening your weaknesses (unless you really want to). There are plenty of people in the world who are good at things you are not. You don't have to be good at everything. Focus on *your* strengths.

You Don't Have to Change Everything

Remember this *second KEY—anything* is possible. When you are trying to create change in your life, keep in mind that you are part of complex systems. Ecosystems in nature are an example of complex systems. Everything in that system from the trees to the bacteria is part of a whole and they have various impacts on one another. A change in one part of the system impacts other parts and the changes can be far ranging and not easy to predict. It all works together.

As you and your life are part of complexity, there are all sorts of things that affect your life and all sorts of ways you impact other parts of the system. When you are dealing with making positive change, remember that shifting anything in yourself and your life towards what you want will impact all other aspects, inside you and in your relationships as well. It can be a relief to understand that you won't have to change everything. Many problems will fall away as you focus on changing just one thing. Pick the area that you are most interested in or that will have the strongest impact in your life. Because of interconnectedness, as soon as you make a shift, everything else in your life and world will shift too. You won't always know how things will change, but they will and if you are moving towards positive intentions, the changes will be for the better. If you pay attention and grow from what you learn, you will find delightful and even surprising possibilities opening in your life.

Anything is possible when you access and own the wholeness of who you are and remember that the universe is far too complex for your rational mind to understand by itself. Be curious and patient and keep noticing what's different. And remember to laugh and play, because possibility is very playful!

Second Key: Things to Try

1. Practice "dropping into the field of your heart". Notice where your awareness is right now. It might be in your head, somewhere else in your body, or even out of your body. Imagine bringing that awareness into the place of your heart center in the middle of your chest in whatever way works for you. Use your creativity to find a way that feels fun and right for you. Notice how it feels and what happens when you are in the field of your heart.

2. Try asking open-ended questions like "What else is possible?" "How could this be different?" and "What else could I notice?" and pay attention to what comes forward.

3. Next time you feel uncertain about something in your life, practice being present to the uncertainty and staying there for a while. Notice how you feel and what you want to do. What is the balance between sitting with this uncertainty and taking action?

The Third Key:
Find Your Purpose and Passion

"Passion can transform the mind, body and spirit...Passion can align you with the wisdom of nature and the power of what is in your heart."

Jo Lynne Valerie

Purpose is a calling and is based on what you value. It's why you are here and it gives your life meaning and direction. Your purpose is persistent and keeps checking in with you throughout your life. It actually changes as your values and interests change. It feels good to think about and live from purpose and how it gives to others. Purpose brings forward inner qualities like self-reliance, courage, enthusiasm and creativity and it motivates and compels you to take action.

Passions are the things you love learning about, doing and teaching. Passions can make your purpose come alive—they are the ways you live your purpose. They are your unique gifts, talents or blessings but they are rarely logical, linear or rational. More often they are creative and connected to imagination. They can show up in all sorts of ways: fixing something that isn't working, gardening, making a financial spreadsheet on your computer, or reading certain sorts of books.

Some passions are very familiar to you and others may be buried in your unconscious mind waiting to be discovered (or re-discovered). They are buried because you may have a belief or someone has suggested that they aren't worthwhile or are silly things to spend time on. It takes courage to be authentic and to take the risks necessary to own your passions and make them part of your life. Living from your passion takes stepping outside of the boxes of conformity and expectations that you may have been in for a long time.

Doors open when you start to follow your passion. Your unconscious mind gets the message that what you are now focusing on is important and it will go to work to help you, even when you're still a little unsure. The strength of your desire and your emotions gives the message that it is really important and your unconscious dives in to help make it happen. People and resources show up to help you, synchronicities occur and momentum builds.

I like using the term genius to describe people's unique passions, gifts or skills. When you are living from your genius and following your passions and purpose, work doesn't feel like work. Take a moment to think about and write down what you are doing when time flies by and you are feeling most alive and captivated. That's your genius. You naturally feel generous and want to share what you do so easily and effectively. It's not about getting something back for what you give— yet in the end you always do. When you aren't living from your genius, you may find yourself caught up in how much money you are making or how you think you appear to others rather than what you are passionate about and how you can help others. You may feel frustrated or tired. You'll lack enthusiasm. You might be excellent at what you do and people still love what you do for them, but it doesn't move you.

What would it be like for you to spend more of your time living from your passions and your genius? What now limits your ability to follow them? Do you trust that your gifts are important and are part of what the world needs? Would you have them otherwise? I've been caught in the deadening trap of no longer living from my genius. No longer being willing or able to stay in that stuck place has pushed me to make choices to leave stable and successful relationships, jobs and businesses to go into the unknown of following my spiritual longings, educational opportunities and creating work that calls once again on my passion and allows me to live from my purpose. I've found it hard to let go of things like work that brought me high praise, loyal clients and money even though I knew I was no longer inspired by that work. Sometimes it's edgy and uncomfortable to create big life changes *and* it's always been worth the challenge of stepping beyond my comfort zone and fear of failure. Happiness, learning and abundance always follow when I live from my genius.

I love to teach and facilitate. It is a privilege and honor to listen to and acknowledge others' life stories and to encourage their growth. My purpose of personal and spiritual growth and helping others to make positive change has taken many forms over the years—health and healing, management and leadership, organizational change, yoga, cohousing development, teaching and coaching—but the thread of purpose is always there. It drives me to keep learning, trying new things and serving others. I've had to make some courageous steps in my life to follow the urgings of my purpose. In working with others, I've experienced many powerful examples of how discovering purpose and passion and living from them with enthusiasm create amazing positive changes.

Purpose and passion are strong *KEYs* to making effective changes in your life and in the world. It feels good to live from them. Find the courage to discover these in yourself, follow where they lead, then bring what you have to offer to others and the world. Your unique gifts are needed now more than ever.

Third Key: Things to Try

1. Write a list of your hobbies, interests, fascinations and passions—what you love to do, learn, and teach to others.

2. Get into a relaxed receptive state and write about these questions:
   - Who are the people who need my genius, my gifts? Who am I here to serve?
   - When I'm living my purpose, how are others transformed by what I offer?

3. Write about what you would do if time, money or health was no issue and you could do whatever you want with your life. What would you do?

The Fourth Key:
Know Your Mind and Beyond

"The mind creates those things that exist." Terry Tempest Williams

The power of the human mind is absolutely…well, mind blowing! I know that some days it may not feel like you have great mind powers (I have days like that too!)—But we're talking huge capacity here. It's just that a lot of your genius is hidden much of the time. Would you like to be able to access it more? Keep reading.

Have you ever felt of two minds? Well, you might, because you do have two sorts of minds—the conscious mind, which you are aware of in your daily life, and your unconscious or subconscious mind that is everything else going on. These two kinds of mind have very different functions. Although you are mostly aware of the conscious mind, it's what you're not aware of in the unconscious that drives most of what happens in your life. When you get your unconscious mind in sync with your conscious mind, anything is possible. But if you think you want something consciously and your unconscious mind isn't in agreement with it, you will have great difficulty making it happen. If you want to make significant changes in your life, your two minds must be in agreement and working together.

Let's explore some of the qualities and differences of each of these minds. The ***conscious mind*** perceives through your five senses and is designed for logic and rational reasoning. It can quickly process up to about 40 or 50 bits of information per second and it's where organizing, day-to-day decisions, language and activities happen. It's a serial processor—one thing (or bit) at a time—and it considers things in linear or cause and effect relationships. The conscious mind focuses on past and future, not what is actually going on at the present time. It's often associated with the left-brain, although that is not completely accurate as there are individual variations in brain function and connections and, hey, no one really knows where mind actually exists! It isn't a tangible thing like a body part; you can do surgery on the brain, but not the mind (although at times that might sound like a good option!).

The **unconscious mind** is sometimes thought of as connected more to the right hemisphere of the brain, but that's also not an accurate picture for something so vast and complex. Your unconscious mind handles things that happen under the level of your usual awareness—functions of body systems, instinctual processes, unnoticed perceptions and thoughts, habits and automatic reactions and what we call intuition. It's where your personality and self-image are stored. It's the storehouse of beliefs, memories, automatic skills and unconscious feelings or emotions including hidden phobias and concealed desires. How you feel about your day is happening mostly at the unconscious level, and instinctual and habitual reactions arise from here.

The unconscious mind passes on information to the conscious mind, but it can just as easily conceal or withhold information it doesn't think is safe for you to know. The conscious mind can only access what's in the unconscious mind if the unconscious is willing to disclose it. Some say you will only get what you are ready for. The unconscious decides if you are ready to deal with an old issue. When it thinks you are, it may then present it to your conscious mind. Your interest in what's in your unconscious will encourage it to share.

As the domain of the emotions, the unconscious mind can repress or bring forward stored emotions into conscious awareness.

Because they are part of the unconscious mind, emotions sometimes take people by surprise, popping up as if "out of the blue".

The unconscious mind processes in symbols and metaphors, not in language. Think about what a night dream is like. With all the strange things that happen in them, dreams don't necessarily make sense to your conscious mind. They are happening in the symbolic language of the unconscious mind. It takes practice and attention to start to understand the unique symbolism of your unconscious mind.

The unconscious mind is a parallel processor, meaning it considers relationships between things as wholes and systems in non-linear ways. One of the most interesting things about the unconscious mind is the amount of data it can handle compared to the conscious mind. Estimates are that it can process in the range of 4.2 million to trillions of bits of information per second (compare that to the 40 or 50 bits per second mentioned earlier for the conscious mind). Some say the conscious mind is like the tip of the iceberg and down underneath, the mass of the unconscious mind floats out of sight influencing everything in your life. It's estimated that the unconscious mind is responsible for over 99% of what you think, feel, believe and how you act.

It might surprise you to learn that what's happening unconsciously always has more power over your thinking and behaviors than your conscious mind. It doesn't matter how much you try to figure out or rationalize something, if there is incongruence between the conscious and unconscious mind, what's in the unconscious will win out every time. Because the unconscious has a profound impact on everything you think and do, you will need to make changes at that level to make lasting positive change in your life.

It's important to know that whatever you focus on, the unconscious mind will take that as direction or instruction to find the quickest, most effective way to get it done. It will do its best to make you aware of and deliver *whatever you are focusing on.* It likes the path of least resistance so it will find the easiest way. It's also a bit like a dog with a bone; it will keep chewing down to the marrow until it's got what it wants. In this way, the unconscious is programmed to keep trying and seeking for more. That can be a blessing or a curse depending on what you are focusing on. Whether it's what you want or what you don't want and are trying to avoid, the unconscious mind is working doggedly to make that happen for you. Through your thinking's focus, that's the direction you are giving the unconscious mind.

The unconscious follows orders like a servant. It relates any information it receives to your consciousness directly, yet it makes no logical, moral or ethical judgments. It leaves that to your conscious mind. It can't even differentiate what is real from what is not. That's why you can get so engaged and emotional about things that are imagined fiction, like movies and particularly your own stories about what's going on around you. Even though you know consciously that it's likely not real, you can't easily control your emotions because your unconscious mind takes the stories to be as real as anything else.

While the conscious mind is busy chatting away to you in words— and quickly editing as it goes—the unconscious mind is taking everything in and recording it without editing. It takes what you say literally and it doesn't understand negatives like "I don't want", or "not". If you say to yourself "I don't want to be depressed", the unconscious picks up on the words and images for depressed. It starts scanning for how you are depressed and brings to your attention other depressing things and people. Your depression will increase and you will notice it more. How depressing! If you focus on what you *do* want—to be happy, fulfilled, or whatever it is— that's what your unconscious will be directed to generate. It's a choice, but one that takes practice to change. You are re-writing well established patterns and brain wiring.

Children start out highly creative and able to access the qualities of both the conscious and unconscious minds. Because socialization and education have strong preferences for rational and logical conscious thoughts, at a young age most people lose the ability to easily access their unconscious mind and its creativity. Think about how that would result in the compliant, rule-bound people that some politicians, religions and corporations might prefer. When you return to using your whole mind, conscious and unconscious together, you gain both more creativity *and* control over your own destiny. You can choose where and when you want to conform and follow societal rules that were set up to maintain community stability, harmony and control but that may reduce useful individual differences within the community.

What is the *Key* to effectively using your conscious and unconscious minds together? The conscious mind senses, perceives and gives meaning to the images and experiences generated by the unconscious. There is a feedback loop between them. The unconscious mind is most present when you are relaxed, open and accepting. Creative processes like visualizing, singing, body movement and feeling, journaling or drawing can help you access your unconscious mind and intuition. It takes practice to allow that symbolic language to come forward, but the more you connect with your unconscious mind, the easier it becomes. It also takes practice to trust that your unconscious mind will only bring forward what you can handle and that it is an incredible reservoir of useful information unique to you.

If you tap into what's there and then use your conscious mind to explore it, this cooperative use of your whole mind will help you understand yourself in a deeper way. It's also a way that groups can find consensus solutions for community issues and decisions rather than setting fixed rules that limit possibility. You can use this knowing of your two minds to live a life that's congruent with your purpose and passions. It's why this *Fourth Key* is so important in making lasting positive change.

While we're on this subject of mind, we can dip into what is "beyond mind". The sages of all traditions refer to sources of infinite possibility, knowledge and guidance that are beyond mind. You might call this Infinite or Universal Energy, Source, Divine, God, Light, the Sea of Awareness, or any term that helps you get a handle on something that's really beyond name and form. You are part of all of that. You *are* that. You are not the solid mass you think you are. Quantum physics and ancient spiritual traditions are clear that everything, including you, is made up of patterns of light or sound vibration and information and that everything is connected as part of the same stuff. Amazing, isn't it? You connect to Source (again, put your own words in here) through your unconscious mind, your heart as well as your thoughts and intentions.

Everything you think and feel gets picked up as vibration by the universe and gets reflected back to you through your experiences and the feelings in your body. Whatever you focus on will be sent back to you in some form, like an echo. Like the unconscious mind, Source is neutral and will follow your wishes. When you feel positive about yourself, life and others, you will get more of that back. If you focus or put your attention on something you don't want, you'll likely feel badly and you'll get more of that coming back. Like it or not, that's what you've asked for.

How do you feel and what happens when you are holding an intention for compassion or love versus blame or revenge? They have very different feelings and results, don't they? So the FOURTH KEY thing to remember is to *focus your mind on what you want*!

Fourth Key: Things to Try

1. Take a few deep breaths, ask your body to relax, focus on the place of your heart and hold an intention for a universal quality like love, compassion, or beauty. Notice what you feel and what happens. Try different intentions and notice the differences in your body and emotions.

2. Watch your dreams, which come from your unconscious mind. Write your dreams down (or record them—I use a portable recording device and transcribe them later) and learn how to explore the symbols and messages that are a rich source of compassionate guidance from within that are available to help you.

3. Many big scientific mysteries have been sorted out when the scientist stopped thinking consciously about it—the answer just popped into awareness. When you are having trouble figuring something out or making a decision, go for a walk or do anything engaging and relaxing. Simply ask your unconscious mind "How can I...?" (Add whatever you want to sort out). Relax, let go of consciously thinking about it (that's where doing something else comes in) and be receptive to what happens when your unconscious mind and universal possibility start exploring your request. Then pay attention to what comes forward, write it down and take action on it.

The Fifth Key:

Get to the Heart of the Matter

"A person's world is only as big as their heart." Tanya A. Moore

Your heart has amazing powers. It is capable of changing your physiology, your feelings and making connections beyond you. Because most people have been taught so much about how to use the head but so little about the heart, it can take practice to learn how to be present in the heart. Once you remember how to do this (it is natural and you already know how), you will find it very useful in making positive change.

Science is exploring the heart in exciting new ways. It turns out that the heart has a mind or intelligence of its own, deeply influencing the ways people perceive and respond to the world. Part of your unconscious resources, the heart is actually a complex, self-organized information-processing center with its own functional brain that communicates with the brain in your head. It profoundly affects intelligence, awareness and most body systems and ultimately determines the quality of your life. Worth paying attention to, don't you think?

The Institute of Heart Math (www.heartmath.org) is on the leading edge of research around the role of the heart in our lives and health. Scientists have found that the rhythm of the heart reflects what is going on in people emotionally and physiologically. Negative emotions lead to disorders of the heart rhythm and of the autonomic nervous system, negatively affecting the body as a whole. When people learn how to increase the coherence in rhythmic patterns of heart rate, perceptions change and stress reduces. Positive emotions create coherent, harmonic heart rhythms that balance the nervous system and help other organ systems work more comfortably and efficiently.

Like so many people in our western culture, I was taught to be rational and logical and to be cautious about what arose from my heart. It has taken practice for me to shift out of the masculine ways of knowing revered by our culture (logic, independence, objectivity, reason, and order) and find balance in the use of my head and heart.

Heart-based ways of knowing are intuitive and are often thought of as feminine. These heart ways require you to include feelings and to be open and receptive to others. Coming from the heart, people see things in wholes rather than parts. This broader heart view is inclusive of multiple inputs and possibilities and focuses on cooperation rather than competition. There is a concern with caring and nurturing of self and other and with exploring relationships between things and people.

Much to the detriment of all peoples, creatures and the environment, our culture downgrades and dismisses heart based knowing. It can be viewed with suspicion or distain in the worlds of science, politics and business. People who come from the heart are sometimes considered flakey or overly emotional. Like many others, you may have been discouraged from following the longings and wisdom of your heart and encouraged to think logically.

Through my later childhood into early adulthood, I leaned towards masculine or rational approaches to thinking. I studied sciences in university, and was proud of my efficiency and apparent clarity of thought. I was sure that if I only worked hard enough, my life would be fulfilling, happy and successful. I kept things of my heart on a short leash and in my control. As I entered into my late twenties, it gradually sunk in that this way of living from my head didn't make me happy and didn't feel complete.

I started to explore spirituality, art and expressive movement. I learned to access intuition and other forms of guidance by using dreams and other symbolic media. My heart wisdom found a natural balance with my already well-practiced intellect. I make choices now by listening to what my heart says and using my head to help figure out how to do it and that has made me a much more whole and happy person.

My deep explorations in the ancient path of yoga, including the study and practice of the Divine feminine, provided a strong foundation for my understanding of my heart. In the last few years, the focus of my quest continues to deepen in the path of the heart and learning how to trust its guidance and wisdom.

Here are a few sources that helped me to explore the heart and what it means to me:

- Yasodhara Ashram (www.yasodhara.net)
- "Awakening the Illuminated Heart" workshops (www.drunvalo.net)
- Richard Bartlett and Melissa Joy (www.matrixenergetics.com)
- Matt Kahn (www.truedivinenature.com)
- Jeddah Mali (www.jeddahmali.com)
- Institute of HeartMath (www.heartmath.org)

As I've mentioned in the earlier Keys, emotions have powerful impacts on thinking, behavior and motivation. Perceptions and emotions are not, as once thought, dictated just by the brain's responses to external stimuli. There are actually more neural connections going *from* the emotional centers (including the heart) to the cognitive ones than the other way around. Current thinking is that external stimuli and feedback to the brain plus internal stimuli from bodily organs and systems to the brain are all part of the information network that determines emotional experience. It's just a lot more complex than anyone used to think.

And that's why it's so useful to understand the part the heart plays in your life. The heart is like a drummer leading the way; it is the most powerful generator of rhythmic information patterns in the human body. With every beat of your heart, complex patterns of information are being sent to the brain and all other organs of your body. When you consciously create internal coherence and harmony, you influence the heart's messages to the brain and body and that will have a profoundly positive influence on body, mind, emotions and spirit. Check out the Heart Math website www.heartmath.org to learn more about how to create coherence.

Other fascinating research explores the heart's cellular memory. There are many documented cases of "Cellular Memory Phenomenon" in which the receiver of a heart transplant suddenly starts having memories that relate to the life of the donor of the heart when they were alive, including things like likes and dislikes and characteristics and behaviors of the donor.

Some say the heart holds the memory from before you came into this life about who you are and what you need to do in this lifetime. Those intuitive messages can direct you when you learn to listen to their wisdom. When you place your attention at the level of your heart, you gain access to a very trustworthy source of internal guidance.

The heart's electromagnetic field is a toroid in shape (like one donut with another smaller donut inside). It is the largest electromagnetic field within the human body—in fact it is about 60 times larger than the energy field of the brain. The electromagnetic field of your heart can be measured and felt by others and extends out five to ten feet, so when you say you are 'touched' by someone, it is likely the field of that person's heart that you are sensing. The frequency that you send out in every direction comes from the unique essence that is you and is generated from your heart. You really can "come from the heart."

Ancient spiritual traditions teach a lot about the heart. Many paths suggest that it is the field of the heart that connects us to Source and to infinite possibility. Sacred teachings about the heart were traditionally handed down orally from teacher to student and were so special (or secret) that they weren't made easy for most people to access. These sorts of teachings are now far more accessible and available. This is true for the traditional teachings of Buddhism and Yoga.

Taking your awareness into your heart can take some practice if you aren't used to going there. Your imagination is a great tool for finding your way into the "field of your heart". Here's where open-ended questions can help. "Where is my awareness located right now? How could I bring that awareness into my heart?" Notice what arises. For example, you might get the notion that some of your awareness is in your head (where a lot of human awareness tends to reside!). Or you might get the sense that part of you is somewhere else in your body, like hanging out in your sore knee or your hungry belly or somewhere else. You might even sense that parts of your awareness are outside your body.

Use your imagination to find a way to bring those parts into your heart. You could find an imaginative way to "drop" the parts in your head into your heart. When I was in Mexico I had fun doing some pretty vertical zip lines. I could imagine those parts in my head harnessed up and taking a quick zip line down into the vast soft space of my heart. Wheee! Or you could simply reach out and take hold of any parts you notice and put them in your heart in a way that works for you. You might get a big butterfly net and catch them that way. Why not? If like me, you wanted to be a cowgirl when you were a kid, it's possible that you could lasso those parts to bring 'em on home.

You get the idea. Be creative and have fun with this. It's doesn't have to be rocket science to get into the field of your heart—in fact it shouldn't be! You probably know lots of ways, like looking at a sunset, cuddling a kitten, thinking of someone you love. It just takes a bit of playful practice. Once you get into your heart, you may notice yourself becoming nicely calm and quiet, and that time itself changes quality. The heart doesn't judge, so the little stuff just doesn't matter so much from this perspective; it will likely feel like a very peaceful and accepting place to be.

There are all sorts of options that open up once you are in your heart. You could just hang out and enjoy the experience. You might ask some questions you are seeking to answer, like what is the purpose of my life, what gives my life meaning, or what are my next steps? You could take some time to meditate or do another spiritual or centering practice known to you. You might use some healing practices. Remember to use this heart time in service to the world and for your own evolution. This hurting world really needs all the heart energy you can muster.

Here's a recent example of followed the longing of my heart and what resulted when I used that to direct my head. Ever since I was a child, the first and middle names chosen for me at birth (Sharon Esther) didn't feel like they belonged to me. I didn't like them but didn't know what to change them to and I didn't want to change them more than once. I wanted to make a choice I could be happy with for years to come. In the fall of 2013, after at least a decade of thinking more seriously about a name change, I had dream about choosing a new name and decided to take action.

My name change required the inspiration and direction of my heart and the abilities of my head in order to research and manage details. I did a lot of research about name change and numerology (the head part got right into it) and also reflected on the internal messages regarding my name choices before I settled on a name (the heart likes this part). I talked to my parents and partner about my intentions and was fortunate that they were supportive of this big shift. I consulted with the Kabalarian Society in Vancouver (www.kabalarians.com), experts in Pythagorean numerology, who help people find balanced names to support their purpose and destiny. I also consulted a numerologist who helped me to include the more mystical Chaldean system. I bounced my name ideas off close friends that I knew could be honest with me and I explored the symbolic meanings of the names I was considering. After I decided on a name, I went through all the detailed legal steps to make the change, which certainly required the organized and logical approach of my head.

Since making a legal name change to Sohlea Rico (I pronounce my first name Solay), I feel different. I've noticed a softening of ambitious parts that strived to be earnest, hard working, successful and upright. I am still willing to work hard for things that matter to me but I find myself thinking more consciously about what I really want and have less interest in doing things because I get some idea that I should. I feel more at ease and accepting of self and others. I'm more light-hearted. I sense that I no longer have anything to prove and feel relief about that. If you want to know more about my name change process, you'll find an article on my blog www.guidingpositivechange.com called "What's in a Name? I Changed Mine".

Remember to take your awareness to your heart on a daily basis and to seek a balance between your concrete rational and your expansive irrational parts—head and heart. They work best as a team!

Fifth Key: Things to Try

1. Notice where you are right now. In your head? Your heart? Somewhere else in your body? Somewhere outside of your body? Several places at once?

2. Ask yourself "If I knew how to bring my awareness into my heart right now, how could I do that?" Notice what comes forward and try it out. Find your own way into your heart.

3. Notice what it feels like to be in your heart. Go there as often as you can and stay for as long as you wish. It's a great place to be!

The Sixth Key:
Discover What You Really Want

"It's a helluva start, being able to recognize what makes you happy."
Lucille Ball

Do you know what you actually want in your life? Once you do, can you follow those longings with passion and purpose? Or are you trying to follow the "right" paths, the ones others suggest you're "supposed to" follow? Do you worry that if you don't make the best choices your life will never turn out right? Does fear of making a wrong choice ever immobilize you from taking action?

It's crucial in making positive change that you move towards what *you* want, not what someone else wants for you. In my early adulthood, like many of my peers, I went to university, got married, bought a house, and entered a stable career. I don't remember thinking much at the time about which parts of my life were what I wanted and which were based on external expectations. Like most people, I tried to please others by fitting in. Some of my choices even went against gut feelings that they weren't right for me. It's interesting that none of those choices have lasted. The choices I make based on what *I* really want and what my heart knows have always *felt* right. Those heart based choices have made me happy, even when they went against others' expectations.

Clients or students sometimes tell me that they don't know what they want. I understand from my experience why they say that, but when they start to look inside and ask questions from a place of curiosity about what they want, they find out that they actually *do* know. It is inside of them, but the internal knowledge of what they want has been crowded out by beliefs and external expectations.

The unconscious mind is actually a great storehouse of memories and information about what you want. It will pass on to your conscious mind what it thinks you want now or what could be useful based on your current focus. However, it will only bring forward what it considers safe in the context of your past experiences. If, somewhere inside, you think that what you want is not okay or if you doubt your capability or worthiness to achieve your dream, the unconscious mind may block your progress. Yet if you try to take action on dreams that *aren't* yours, you won't stay motivated enough to make them come true.

Creating positive change means first consciously deciding what *you* actually want, since not knowing what you want could leave you floundering or trying to live up to others' expectations. It's also important to stay flexible and keep your options open at this stage. Should you become too fixated about exactly what you want, you might eliminate useful possibilities. It may be that there are dreams currently beyond your imagination that can take you to amazing places. Try to hold in mind the big picture of *what* you want without getting too set on *how* it should happen. That way, you leave space for creative possibilities to come in. It might be even better than you can imagine!

It feels good to bring your own desires and dreams out of their hidden places, to acknowledge their truth for you and to take action on them. To access the unconscious information about what you want, be creative. Make your explorations fun and learn to accept whatever comes forward with curious interest. This is the time to get all the creative possibilities out of the closet of your unconscious. Tell the rational mind that judges, that there are *no wrong answers* to this process. There is an exercise at the end of this *Key* to help get you started. Enjoy!

Know What You Value

Values are the things that are important to you in life. They reflect who you are and guide where you put your time, energy and money. Values provide motivation. When you think back to a time when you were really motivated, a value was always at the root of it. How you spend your time, energy, and resources greatly impacts what happens in your life and the results you get. If something isn't on your internal list of values, you just can't get motivated about it or it could be too far down your list to get your attention.

Just as many people aren't all that sure about what they want, most people aren't very clear about what they value. This is understandable; many values get installed into the unconscious mind at an age before rational choices could be made about their usefulness. Values get imprinted easily in the unconscious mind from birth to age seven when there are few filtering mechanisms. Children absorb ideas, especially those from parents. They are like the kitchen wipe in a television commercial with a never-ending capacity to absorb liquids. What values did you absorb in your infancy and early childhood? Do they continue to serve you well? Which do you want to let go of? What other values might now serve you better?

Between the ages of seven and fourteen, children model themselves after popular peers as well as Internet, television, and book characters. The values of those models may or may not be helpful as you become an adult. For example, a value that tells you that only the most beautiful people are likeable and successful might make plastic surgeons and diet authors rich, but it probably won't contribute to your happiness, especially as you age.

After fourteen, youth begin to adopt their own values and are less likely to adopt something just because other people tell them it's cool. Beyond this stage (which I presume you are in if you are reading this book), you can decide what values will move you towards what you want in your life. However, many people have never taken the time as adults to clarify what's most important to them. If you don't know what you value and you are trying to live up to societal or parental values that don't matter to you, you will find yourself frustrated and going nowhere, maybe even sabotaging your own efforts at change. Taking the time to figure out what you value and which of those values are most important to your life dreams is crucial in making positive change.

Conflicts may arise between your various values, leaving you confused about which ones to follow. For example at one point, my values around environmental sustainability led me to believe that driving somewhere to go for a walk by myself was wasteful and unnecessary. I would go for walks mostly from my home and grumble inside when I saw another neighbor drive off in their car to go for a walk. But I also value time in nature by myself. When I got clear about this value conflict between sustainability and my need for time alone in nature, I realized that having time alone in nature was being subjugated by my sustainability value. I gave myself permission to drive more often to walk alone in nature. Now I do some of each. I often walk or cycle straight from home or carpool with others, but occasionally I do drive to a special place when I want to be alone in nature. An unexpected positive side effect beyond the time alone in nature is that I do less grumbling inside and out about others' driving preferences!

This leads into how values become criteria for evaluating your own and others' actions. After an event, you evaluate whether or not it was worthwhile based on your values. For example, if you value spiritual development and you decide to sleep-in most days instead of getting up early to meditate as you planned, you will likely feel guilty, because you haven't lived up to your spiritual development value and plan. If someone else does something that is not in keeping with your values, you will likely judge their behavior as not good enough or inappropriate. The tension and stress around judgment creates both division and suffering.

When you start thinking and writing about values and what's important to you, it can be disconcerting to discover the value conflicts and judgments that affect your decisions, actions and relationships. It can be like the story of the emperor with no clothes, as we shed illusions about how we think we are in the world. While it can offer lessons in humility, it can also be a temporary blow to a guarded self-image. So it's useful to consider what you already have achieved in your life and what does work well. A list of your internal strengths and the external resources you can count on is a powerful tool in creating positive change. Knowing where you've come from and where you are now helps you to positively imagine the possibility and process of change.

Choose What to Believe

What you believe generates most of what happens in your life. A belief is your idea of what is true about your values. Beliefs are also the rules about what's important to you. Beliefs generate how you feel, how you behave, what you are attracted to and which people and situations you attract to yourself. Beliefs are at the core of how you show up in the world.

Beliefs come out of values. A number of beliefs will be connected to each of your values. I like to think of this like a clothesline. The line is a value and all the things pinned on and hanging on that line underneath are the beliefs. For example, if you value family, you will have a number of beliefs about families and in particular about *your* family hanging on that line. Imagine all these beliefs hanging on the line: "Families stick together", "Blood is thicker than water", "You can trust family", "Without family life has no meaning" "You can choose your friends but not your family" and so on. Take a moment to think about what other beliefs might hang on your family line. Because beliefs and values are so connected, problems related to beliefs often clear up when you clear up problems with values.

Beliefs are the "why" and "how" to everything that happens in your life, and beliefs either positive or negative, can become self-fulfilling prophecies. Yet people are often not aware of this, because so many beliefs are unconscious and were established in early childhood. Based on your early interactions and experiences, especially with your primary caregivers, you developed beliefs about yourself and your relationship to the rest of the world. Most of these early beliefs are then carried unconsciously throughout life. People seldom question these beliefs and whether or not they are still useful, yet they impact everything that happens to them.

You will focus on whatever you believe to be true. This focus serves as an instruction to your unconscious mind to notice it and support it happening in your life. It also serves as an instruction to the universe to bring it to you. If you believe the world is a safe and trustworthy place, your unconscious mind will find evidence to support that belief; those are the sorts of situations, people and experiences you will attract into your life and you will feel safe as a result. Yet if you believe that the world is dangerous and unsafe, your unconscious mind will show you how that is true and you will be watching for and noticing all the ways the world is not safe. With this focus, unsafe situations will turn up regularly in your life.

What's useful to know is that beliefs are not inherently true or false. Different people hold different beliefs about the same things and they all think their beliefs are true. While all people will unconsciously find ways to support their beliefs, this results in no end of conflict in the world, with people regularly killing each other in support of their beliefs.

Beliefs shape your life, because you make your life conform to what you believe. When you think something is true, you'll figure out a way to be right about it, or at least to make it look like you're right. People unconsciously *delete* knowledge that doesn't agree with what they believe to be true. For example, if you believe that climate change doesn't exist, you will disregard the masses of scientific data that indicates otherwise.

Do you think your senses give you a true picture of what's going on? Unfortunately, it's just not so. People automatically *distort* the information coming in through their senses to reinforce the "truth" of their beliefs. If you believe that no one likes you, for instance, you may misinterpret or underplay acts of friendship from others in order to support your belief that you are not likable. You might think they are acting friendly in order to get something from you. When others see you act in ways that confirm your beliefs, they automatically comply with your expectations. Yet if you believe that you are friendly and warm, you will attract and be attracted to others and to situations that confirm this belief. People comply with the messages you are unconsciously putting out based on your beliefs about yourself.

Have you heard of cognitive dissonance? You will find yourself very uncomfortable when your beliefs and what you actually think or do in your life are not consistent. For example, if you believe in honesty in relationships but you are having an affair and lying to your spouse about it, you will feel the discomfort of cognitive dissonance. You will likely find ways to convince yourself that your actions aren't actually all that bad and are even justified. Very few people own up to others about their weaknesses and mistakes, because cognitive dissonance makes it so uncomfortable to first admit them to self.

Some of your beliefs are powerfully self-enhancing; others are woefully outdated. Although they may have served you in the past, they now cause you pain and suffering. Significant negative emotional experiences, trauma, or wounding create beliefs that are not usually helpful. For example, the trauma of being told that you are stupid or bad or ugly as a child will have installed negative beliefs in your unconscious mind. Traumatic and negative experiences carry an emotional charge and the power of that charge takes your focus to what you don't want. If you had a past experience involving fear and still carry the emotional charge of that experience, you will automatically watch out for what caused the fear in the first place. When you focus on the thing that you are afraid of, your unconscious mind will be watching out for it and will notice and create even more of it. Since your unconscious mind creates or attracts whatever you focus on, as long as you hold the same beliefs, you will get the same results. When you add strong emotion to whatever you are focused on, the unconscious thinks you want it as soon as possible and it will go to work even faster to make it happen!

It's crucial in creating the changes you want for your life and in the world to hold your attention on what you want and to stop paying attention to what you don't want. Remember the title of this book: *"It Ain't Easy But It's Worth It"*? This is sometimes where the going gets tough…yet it really is worth making change in your beliefs about yourself!

A first step to having beliefs that support what you now want is to discover what it is that you currently believe. The next step is to figure out which of those beliefs don't serve you well and the final step is to install beliefs that will. No amount of positive thinking, affirmations, spiritual practice, or anything else will work to full potential until you remove beliefs that aren't serving you and install positively supportive beliefs. If you aren't creating the life you want, it's likely because some of your beliefs are outdated, do not serve you positively, or are self-defeating and need to be upgraded. When it comes to beliefs, if you can't embrace them as supportive, then it's time to replace them.

It's useful to remember that these unhelpful beliefs are mostly very old and well entrenched. It can take some time for new, supportive beliefs to feel like they are yours. When installing new beliefs, you may have to "fake it 'til you make it". Pretend, think and act as if you believe what you want to believe until it becomes more habitual. Choose the beliefs you want to have, based on the outcome you desire. To install a new belief, focus on it as often as possible and in every way you can think of. There are useful techniques from various spiritual traditions and from approaches like Neuro Linguistic Programming that focuses on positively directing the unconscious mind.

It's exciting to know that by continually updating your beliefs, you can take responsibility for achieving the outcomes you value in your life. You are the one in charge and when you begin to believe that you are the creator of what happens in your life, things do change for the better. You really do discover that anything is possible!

Thresholds and Limits

Given the positives of living your purpose and passion, you'd think we'd all be living from that place. However, the unconscious mind places limits on your ability to follow purpose and passion. People have unconscious upper limits or thresholds for how much of anything they can handle—love, health, success, money or joy, for instance—before they start to feel unsafe. When you get near or go over one of these unconscious thresholds, you will automatically find ways to take the pressure off and go back to where you feel safe. You will unconsciously sabotage what you consciously want. These thresholds and limits get created based on beliefs. For example, if you carry an upper limit about how much happiness or joy you believe you can have in your life, each time you start to feel really happy, you will find a way to go back to where you feel secure or comfortable again—even though there is less happiness there. You might find yourself arguing with someone or noticing or thinking about something you are unhappy about.

I have had a threshold for financial abundance and success. I have a tendency to believe that more success will make me too busy, that I will lose time for other things I love to do, or that my life will become stressfully out of balance. Writing this book took courage and determination (and more time than I expected it to) in part because of these beliefs. My upper limit for success reared its head from time to time in the process of writing. Continuing on and working against the stream of those beliefs has raised my threshold for success and helped me to see success in a different light—as an internal sense of living the life I want to live rather than an external set of conditions.

In my experience as a therapist and teacher, I've seen many examples of people making positive changes and then suddenly 'something' takes them back to an old way. They break a leg or have a big fight with their spouse or stop practicing what got the positive changes happening in the first place. It's much easier to notice when someone else hits a threshold and finds a way to go back to the familiar than it is to see it in yourself. There are many sorts of behaviors that may appear when you are reaching your threshold. They may include: finding reasons why you can't do something, worrying, blaming others, being critical, deflecting positive feedback, lying, arguing, getting sick or having an injury. Watch for these signs in yourself and think about what's really happening, what's at the root of it. Awareness of thresholds will help you to test them and have the courage and determination to "pick yourself up, dust yourself off and start all over again".

To summarize this *Sixth Key*, it is useful to know what you want, to focus on that and at the same time be flexible and open to whatever possibilities are emerging, trusting that they will take you where you want to go—or to something even better!

Your values and beliefs drive what happens in your life so it is important in making positive change to understand what they are and how they operate. You *can* let go of conflicts in values, install the beliefs that support your dreams, test limiting thresholds and create the full life of purpose and possibility that is your birthright.

Sixth Key: Things to Try

1. Get into a relaxed and receptive state of mind and write as quickly as possible about what you would do if you only had a certain amount of time left to live: a year, a month, a week, a day. This exercise can reveal with clarity what's most important to you.

2. Get into the habit of noticing beliefs and what beliefs are behind what happens in your life. Catch your "broken records"—things you say about yourself and your life that are self-limiting. Stop complaining immediately and change the story and belief to one that serves you positively.

3. Focus on your strengths rather than on trying to improve your weaknesses. Write out lists of your assets, which could include your strengths, qualities, skills, knowledge base, relationships and connections as well as your material assets. Remember and draw on these when you want to make positive change. Think about how these resources can move you towards what you want.

The Seventh Key:
Focus on What You Want

"We can always choose to perceive things differently. You can focus on what's wrong in your life, or you can focus on what's right."

Marianne Williamson

If you've read The *Sixth Key*, you'll probably understand that you generate most of what happens in your life through what you focus on. Since you are generating it, you are in charge. You can create something different if you don't like what's happening. Now that's empowering!

Put in Neuro Linguistic Programming (NLP) terms, this is how you generate what happens:

1. Information comes in from an external event through your five senses (and likely your intuition, too).

2. The incoming sensory information is subjected to a variety of filters, including your attitudes, beliefs, values, personality and thinking patterns, memories, cultural expectations, and language.

3. As the incoming information gets filtered, some of it also gets tossed out. What is *deleted* is the stuff you aren't interested in or whatever goes against your beliefs or values. Some gets *distorted*—changed to suit what you would prefer it to be so it is congruent with your beliefs and values. Other information gets

generalized and put into a category with something you have previously experienced, whether or not that's appropriate now.

4. What's left after all this unconscious filtering and changing of the incoming information is the "internal representation" of what you've experienced. It's not the facts, not what actually happened, but your personal interpretation of the information—what's true about the event for you.

5. These *internal representations*, or interpretations of what happens in life, drive your "state": your behaviors, thoughts, emotions, speech, actions and interactions with others.

6. Your state greatly influences the results you get in your life.

It's important to remember that this filtering and representing process happens mostly in your unconscious mind. These processes happen automatically within milliseconds, yet they significantly influence your conscious life. It's why it is important to change these automatic and generally unconscious programs if you want to change your life. When you accept full responsibility for your life and take the time to question the filters more consciously, you give yourself the power to change your emotions, feelings, what you notice and what you attract. It empowers you to start generating what you really want in your life.

Your internal representations developed and evolved throughout your childhood. They served you well by creating safety for you as a vulnerable young human. As a child, you unconsciously shaped reality to conform to what your parents and caregivers wanted so that they would protect you and give you a place to belong. Not only were there these individual influences, there were also broader cultural expectations about how to think, and what to value and believe.

What you already think about and focus on is what you will continue to notice and generate. A number of years ago, my partner and I bought a new car: a light green Toyota Prius. I had never noticed this model much before but after I became an owner, I saw them everywhere. I especially noticed the light green ones. Did a whole fleet of green Prius cars suddenly start driving around my city? Not likely. I just hadn't noticed them before.

So how did my attention shift to green Prius cars? There's an area of the brain called the "reticular activating system" (RAS). It sits above the brainstem at the top of the spinal cord. It's a connector between the more primitive instinctual brain (the brainstem) and the higher brain (cerebral cortex). The RAS is the area where thoughts, internal feelings and outside stimuli converge. It is responsible for many critical functions including sleep and waking, dreams, motivation, breathing, and the beating of your heart.

The RAS takes instructions from your conscious mind (like the image of green Prius cars) and gives them to your unconscious mind. Like the unconscious mind, the RAS does not differentiate what is real from what you imagine. It treats it all the same—as if it were real. It filters out most of the information coming from external sources to enable you to focus on a particular fact, detail or thought, like my focus on green Prius cars over other models and colors. Deleting what's not required for your internal image is necessary. You couldn't possibly pay attention to everything happening all at once in this busy world without going bonkers.

The old advice "be careful what you ask for" is appropriate; you *will* notice and get what you focus on. If you are focusing on what you want, you will most likely notice people, resources, and opportunities that help you create more of them. If you focus on what you don't want, you will notice and draw more of that to you. To make positive changes in your life, you must establish new habits of focusing on what you want and diminish old patterns of focusing on what you don't want. Remember that no matter what you focus on, whether you consciously want it or not, the message will pass from the reticular activating system (RAS) to the unconscious mind. Your unconscious will start scanning for what you are focusing on and help you to notice and generate more of that in your life.

Your RAS and unconscious mind do not understand qualifiers like "not" or "don't". If you think or say, "I'm *not* afraid", the unconscious mind processes the "afraid" part because it gets the image and feelings of it—the symbol of afraid. It starts to direct you to notice how you feel afraid, what there is to be afraid of, and points to others who are also afraid. It's doing just what you've asked it to do—to notice what you are focusing on (in this example, fear).

You've no doubt had the experience of being afraid of something: all your senses go on alert, your breathing becomes shallow and you pay close attention. As you pay attention, your fear increases and your attention focuses even more on what you don't want, making you more afraid. Your conscious mind is pretty useless by now, and now that you've started focusing on it, the fear is hard to stop. If you want to be able to face something that causes you fear, you might try saying to yourself, "I am courageous", or "I am safe, I am okay". Your unconscious mind will start to notice those qualities and will draw those resources both from within and outside of you.

Have you noticed how, when you feel excited about something, things start happening or they proceed more quickly than when something doesn't matter so much to you? You will get what you focus on quicker and more powerfully if you bring strong emotion to it. Your unconscious mind experiences emotion as urgency and it will go to work to generate what you are focusing on more quickly. It will make you aware of the internal resources that will help you get it. You will find yourself attracted to books, movies, and websites that are about that topic you are interested in as well as being drawn to people who know something about the topic. Of course, those sorts of people will also be attracted to you, because you are thinking and talking about their topic of interest.

It all sounds pretty clear and direct, but you may have experienced that it is sometimes easier said than done to focus on and generate what you want in your life. Why is that? Remember that the unconscious mind is also your warehouse of beliefs and memories. If, somewhere in storage, you have an unconscious belief that goes against what you are trying to manifest in your life, it just isn't going to happen. The first job will be to let go of those limiting beliefs (of which you aren't consciously aware) and install beliefs that support what you do want. Sometimes you'll need someone to help you do this, as it's hard to find what you aren't aware of.

For example, perhaps you want to go to college or university but you have an unconscious belief that you aren't smart enough or that it won't be okay with your family. With these beliefs in operation, you are not likely to find the courage and resources to get you there. Your unconscious mind will offer all sorts of reasons why you can't or shouldn't and you'll start to notice evidence to support your limiting belief. Or if you've had a negative or traumatic experience with previous learning, you might find the unconscious power of that memory (or the feelings connected to it) stopping you from moving toward what you want. You may even sabotage your attempts to make that dream happen by doing things like not gathering the money you need or not getting your application in on time.

Your DNA is the other factor that makes it hard to focus on what you want. Humans have survived through the centuries by paying way more attention to what is a potential threat to life than to what is nice and what they want. Humans have a huge survival bias that leads to remembering negative experiences much more than positive ones and to clinging to what has been safe in the past. The people who went out on a limb likely didn't live to pass their genes on to you. Your ancestors and mine were the ones who stayed on alert, played it safe and survived!

What's the trick? How can you use the combination of your conscious and unconscious minds to focus on and manifest what you want in your life? First, you can get to know your unique unconscious mind and learn how to trust its wisdom. It has your best interests in mind and wants to serve you in whatever way it can. When you really want to know, it will be straight and honest in presenting what it contains in order to help you. If you can find ways to tell it what you want, it will find ways to help.

Spend time noticing and bringing in the good things in your life. Stop and smell the flowers more often in order to train your unconscious mind to focus on what you want and what is good. You can do this regularly through the day, as it only takes a minute. Learn the symbolic language of your unconscious and it will start sharing more and more with you in that language. There's a great storehouse of useful information there and you gain access to more of it by paying attention to what it presents. The keener you are to learn about yourself, the more forthcoming your unconscious will become. If you are curious and want to learn, the secrets in your unconscious mind will reveal themselves in the amount you are ready to deal with. However, if you are afraid of what's in there, that material won't come out easily.

The *Seventh Key* thing to remember about generating results that you *do* want in your life is to: "FOCUS ON WHAT YOU WANT" (thus taking your mind off what you don't want). What you pay attention to sends a message to your unconscious mind and to the universe about what you want to create. So be curious and be courageous. Take responsibility for where you put your focus and what you create in your life.

Seventh Key: Things to Try

1. Write a dialogue or conversation between yourself and some aspect of your personality. Psychologist Carl Jung called this process "active imagination". It is one of my favorite ways of talking to my unconscious mind. It's almost like writing a play. For example, you might dialogue with your inner critic to find out more about its purpose for you so that you can know it better. How about finding a useful job for the critic that helps rather than blocking you? You'll need to stay curious in this conversation, avoiding judgment if you want these parts to talk with you.

2. Close your eyes and imagine a time when you felt really good about yourself—a time when you were happily doing what you loved. Notice where the image is in your visual field—the size, brightness or colour. Notice sounds, feelings, tastes or smells. See it all through your own eyes, and then allow that image to disperse. Now create an image of something you want in your life. Put it in the same place as the prior image using the same qualities. See it through your own eyes and add senses that were present in the first image. Run this "movie" every day in your mind's eye, noticing how you feel and what happens in your life. This is an NLP technique called "Mapping Across".

3. Chose something that you've been trying to create that feels blocked. Get into a relaxed, receptive state by taking your attention to your heart. List the beliefs that may be keeping you from what you consciously want. Just being aware of what they are shifts them. Write out a new belief that will help you move towards what you want. Focus on that belief in as many ways as you can. Post it where you can see and read it throughout the day, draw pictures or make a collage of it, or use the practice of the prior exercise to install it in your unconscious mind.

The Eighth Key:
Take Effective Action

"Have a bias toward action - let's see something happen now. You can break that big plan into small steps and take the first step right away."
Indira Gandhi

If you've read some other *KEYS* from this book, you will likely be getting the message that what you focus on makes all the difference to what happens in your life. Your unconscious mind will go to work to help you notice and create more of whatever you are focusing on and the universe will cooperate in mirroring that back to you.

The Five-Step Cycle for Taking Effective Action

The next piece of making your dreams a reality is taking action. With all the ideas coming forward from your unconscious mind about how you can create what you are focusing on, you can now formulate a vision and a plan of what you want to see happen and then step up to the plate and try some of them out. Or you may share a vision with others that you want to take action on together.

To help you understand this cycle of effective action, I'll weave a real life example of the dream I shared with my partner about creating a cohousing community—how we took action, what happened along the way and what the outcome has been.

Many people have great ideas and a vision of what they'd like to see happen. They mean to do something about it, but in fact, only a few take the risks and the actions needed to make their vision a reality. There are great rewards for those courageous enough to take action on their visions. Do you have that courage? I think so!

The following Five Steps will help turn your dreams into reality:

1. Visioning

2. Goal Setting

3. Implementing

4. Feedback & Evaluation (then cycling back to step 5)

5. Take the Next Action.

It's not as hard as you might think!

1. Visioning

Visioning is the ability to creatively imagine and define a desired future or new possibilities that you would like to bring into reality. Visioning goes beyond how you *see* a possibility. Powerful visions include all of your senses—what it will look like, sound like, feel like and perhaps even smell and taste like when it has come into being. The more multi-sensory and clear your imagination of what you want to create, the more inspired you will be in making it happen.

The vision my partner Arlene and I shared back in 2004 was of building and living in a cohousing community in our area in the Comox Valley on Vancouver Island. We had attended some workshops about cohousing a decade before when we lived in Whitehorse, Yukon and the idea had been simmering in our unconscious minds. When the time came for us to move house, the cohousing idea came back to the surface and a vision began to form.

We envisioned a neighborhood of beauty and peace where people of all ages could connect positively with each other. We wanted the privacy and financial security of owning our home combined with opportunities to connect and share resources with like-minded neighbors. Creating a community that fostered personal growth and responsibility along with a lighter footprint on this planet were important considerations.

Life purpose (the *Third Key*) is always an impetus for creating a positive vision of the future. Arlene and I shared a purpose of service in the world through teaching and leadership in personal and spiritual development. We had committed to a life together in the secular world rather than living full time in a spiritual community, so we took a leap of faith to make our vision happen.

When you take action based on your purpose and a compelling vision, people notice you and take you seriously. They gather around you, wanting to get involved. Your enthusiasm is contagious when what you are describing is of value to them. That's what happened as our community vision started to take shape and form. Our enthusiasm and care attracted many people passionate about creating community. As each new person added ideas, the shared vision grew.

Being involved in creating this shared vision of a positive future was exciting and empowering. It brought out the best in people and challenged us to go further. Think of a time where you were either inspired by someone else's vision or you inspired others with yours. What did that feel like? What happened?

Remember that the vision of what you want to manifest will get passed from your conscious to your unconscious mind through your words and images. The more clear and multi-sensory your imagination of your desired future and the more emotion you can put behind it, the more your unconscious mind will take it as instruction that it's what you want. As part of the early visioning process, our group explored what our community could be like—not only through words and descriptions, but also through images and feelings. Several months after we moved into our new community of Creekside Commons Cohousing, we found a collage of images a group of us had made in the early days of the development process. It was amazing to see how similar the houses we now lived in were to the images we had selected several years before.

As part of the process of visioning, it's useful to get clear on *why* you want this thing and what you will gain and lose if you get what you want. Ask yourself what you will see, hear, and feel when you have reached your vision. Imagine what achieving it will do for you and how it will change your life. Determine what resources you now have and what you will need in order to make it happen. With expert help, our cohousing group carefully assessed the feasibility of this project. Once we determined that we could access the resources to make it happen, we went for it.

As your vision becomes clearer, you naturally develop goals and plans for how to reach it. When you make a commitment to your dream and your purpose and believe you are worthy of it, you can select the ideas, direction and resources that will best serve you.

Of course, there's a price to pay for everything you want. To plan and build Creekside Commons, many members, including me, contributed about a half time job worth of unpaid work, including giving every second weekend to the project for over two years. Sometimes we craved time to do other things, but our vision of what this community would be like and how it would change our lives kept us showing up and doing the needed work for the duration of the project.

Flexibility is important, too. Vision is meant to motivate you and others towards a desired future, but how you get there and what it eventually looks like will change as you go along. Sometimes the differences will be little and sometimes what you end up with will have changed significantly from what you originally imagined. Creekside Commons (www.creeksidecommons.net) isn't exactly what I thought it would be, yet it's better now in ways that are far beyond what we thought to include in that early vision.

2. Goal Setting

In the process of developing our cohousing community, goal setting was crucial for keeping a large complex project on track. While we had Ronaye Matthew (www.cohousingconsulting.ca), a talented project manager to thank for a process that kept this complex project on time and on budget, your steps in taking action will likely be simpler. However the same principles for setting goals apply to anything you want to create.

Taking action based on a vision is much more effective and directed when you set clear goals and write them down. A written plan is far more likely to happen than if it stays unformed in your thoughts. This action plan, or set of ideals, gives direction to your unconscious mind to go to work in seeking what you are looking for. It will call your internal qualities forward and will draw people and resources to you. You will naturally put your time, energy and money behind your vision and amazing synchronicities and help will appear.

A well-formed goal is SMART—specific, measurable, attainable, realistic and timely. By writing a goal statement, you gain clarity about what you want and where you want to go. You acknowledge that you are willing to do what it takes to get there. The statement reminds both your conscious and unconscious minds of what you intend to achieved in the time limit you've set.

You can make each goal specific by describing clearly what you will have, as if you've already achieved that goal. Remember that you are giving direction to your unconscious mind, so make sure it knows specifically what you want. If you want a new bicycle, write down what sort of bicycle you are looking for and what factors are most important to you in that selection. If you want more friendships, be specific about how many, with what sorts of people and for what purpose. If you want to develop a positive habit, write down what it is, when you will do it and how it will be in your life when you are doing it.

Your goals need to be attainable and realistic—something that is within the realm of your control. Having a goal to be a gold medal Olympic athlete when you are already in your 40's and have no particular athletic prowess is not likely to happen (but hey, anything is possible!).

It is important to set a time frame for when you want this goal to manifest. Make the time frame realistic yet near enough that it provides some motivation for you to take action and work towards it. There may be a number of steps in your timeframe if the goal is complex and that's just fine.

You'll also need some criteria that will tell you when you've reached your goal. It's useful to write down how you will know when you've got it—what you will have, how it will look, feel, sound (and perhaps taste and smell), and how your life will be different when you have it. Writing about what you will gain will motivate you and writing about what you might lose helps you to realize that there is always a price to pay for what you want—in time, energy, money or giving something up.

Remember that the one thing you can count on is change. While writing it down *is* important, when it comes to planning, sometimes less is more. Even the best-laid plans need to be flexible and adapt to unexpected changes. Over-planning can be the death of a good idea; there needs to be room for it to organically keep developing into something that could be even better.

If you don't know whether to plan more or take action—always take some action. It will bring feedback that tells you more about your plan. As you open up your vision and goals to others, people will provide valuable feedback from their experience and knowledge. From my experience, teams or groups of people working cooperatively tend to make higher quality decisions than individuals. So open up to and ask for the involvement of others early on.

Everything in the universe has a cycle of doing and being. It's important to balance action with time for reflection, patience and waiting. Leave space for other possibilities that may be even more useful to come forward. Your unconscious mind will be processing everything you are thinking about. The best ideas often come when you are doing something else, like going for a walk or taking a shower, or from a dream, a daydream or an idea that forms as you wake up. When a potentially useful idea pops into your head, be sure to write it down or voice record it, even if it's the middle of the night, so you can remember it and consider it later.

3. Implementation

My partner and I decided that our vision for creating a cohousing community was worth exploring further. The best action we could think of was to set up a meeting and gather some people together who might also be interested. As we connected with people, a tip came forward to contact the woman who ended up being our project manager. Despite short notice and a date between Christmas and New Years, she was available to help us design and lead our first meeting. By taking that first action, ideas and feedback came our way and we were able to take next steps as a result.

A key in moving forward with your vision and goals is to take the best action you can think of at the time, knowing that it likely won't be perfect. By doing something, you will set your vision in motion and you'll start getting the feedback you need to tell you if you are on track or not. Then you can make adjustments accordingly. You don't need to reinvent the wheel. Gather what's already out there and apply it. Model people who have already achieved what you want. Focus on your strengths and find support from people who are strong in areas where you are weak.

The most successful people and projects have made many mistakes along the way. If you feel like you've failed or something isn't going well, remember that failure is a normal part of the process and trial and error is how all people learn. Find out how the mistake happened, learn from it and get back on track as soon as you can.

Be open to the help of the universe and guidance from trusted sources inside you and outside. Watch for synchronicities. Call on your whole mind—logic and intuition to be part of the process. Bring in feminine qualities of feeling, being receptive, and cooperating with others. Use creativity, the body, intuition, and be sure to leave space and time for the gestation or digestion of ideas.

4. Feedback and Evaluation

Once you've taken an action, it's useful to be open and receptive to what differences it generates. Try gathering feedback from as many sources as you have available and evaluating the results. Did the action take you in the direction you are seeking? What worked? What didn't work? How could you have done it better? Asking questions cues your unconscious mind to find answers.

When you are evaluating your progress, it's useful to look behind to where you have come from, not ahead to where you want to end up. Our cohousing development meetings always included a list of what had been achieved and what still needed to be done or adapted. Your vision is a big picture and for a time it will be off in the distance. Depending on the size of your vision, it could be some distance away. If you measure your progress by how far you've made it towards your vision, you will likely get discouraged when it seems far away. Your progress can feel tiny relative to the distance left to go.

So measure your progress by where you have come. What have you accomplished this day or week or month? What's different today than yesterday? What worked and what didn't work? What did you learn? Is there something you could do differently to improve? Who could you ask about it? Write your victories and successes down and celebrate them in ways that are fun and meaningful for you. They are just as important as your plans and will help you to stay motivated.

It was vital in our cohousing development project of over two and a half years to watch for the feedback that guided our next steps and to keep track of things like how many new members had signed on, how far along we were in our timeline, where construction was at and so on. Our project manager encouraged us to celebrate our victories regularly. Those fun events helped balance all the work and encouraged us to keep going.

5. Taking the Next Action

Based on the feedback you gather and your evaluation, choose a next step. What's the next thing you can think of that will move you towards your vision and goals? Take that step and then continue the cycle of action, feedback, evaluation, reflection and refining the next action. Learn from your mistakes and keep going. Be flexible as you go along and adapt your goal as needed.

Taking action is a crucial *Key* in making positive change. It is inspiring to create a vision of what you want, make a plan, set some goals and write them down. Be willing to take the best action you can think of and gather feedback about what happened as a result. You can then evaluate where that action has taken you and choose the next action. Keep moving forward, taking step-wise actions, gathering feedback and adjusting your plan accordingly. The amazing capacity of your unconscious mind and the power of the universe will naturally jump in to help. Ask open-ended questions and enjoy taking the time to relax and be receptive to ideas that come forward.

To create what you want in your life will mean staying committed to your vision and goals. Bring forward your enthusiasm and excitement, be patient and positive and trust that what you are dreaming of (or something even better) will happen. Above all, remember to have fun with what, after all, is your precious life!

Eighth Key: Things to Try

1. Write about a time that you set and reached an important goal. How did it happen? What actions did you take? How did it feel? How has it influenced your life?

2. Answer any or all of these questions to define a goal for yourself:

   - What do I want specifically?

   - Why do I want this goal? What will I gain if I get it? What will I lose?

   - What *will happen* if I *do* get it? What *won't happen* if I *do* get it?

   - What *will happen* if I *don't* get it? What *won't happen* if I *don't* get it? (I know, these can be confusing—go slowly)

   - Is this feasible? Do I have the power to influence this area?

   - Can I initiate and maintain this goal on my own or do I need help?

   - Where, when, how and with who do I want it?

   - What will I see, hear, and feel when I have it?

   - What will achieving my goal allow me to do? What are the rewards?

   - What do I intend to give in exchange for attaining this goal?

   - What's the maximum time I will allow for the attainment of my goal?

   - What resources do I need to reach this goal? What resources do I already have?

   - Have I ever done this before? What do I know about it? Has anyone else ever done it? How can I find out about how they did it?

3. Write out a goal statement in the first person. I _____ (your name) will commit to... (The goal).

   - What you want specifically

   - What you intend to give for attaining this goal

   - The maximum time you will allow for the attainment of your goal

The Ninth Key:
Stay the Course

"Life is not about how fast you run or how high you climb but how well you bounce." Vivian Komori

I grew up in the Canadian prairies with snowy, slippery winter roads and many opportunities to explore traction—or the lack of it. To stay the course and keep moving forward in a Canadian winter, it helps when you have good tires and you slow down and steer into a slide, not away from it. Staying the course in personal growth and development requires the same things—a foundation that gives you traction, a slow and steady approach and going *towards* the tough places rather than steering away from them. And you may need to accept that there will sometimes be some slipping.

The foundation that gives you traction is your life experience. It's all the things you've learned along the way about the world, about who you are and about what works and doesn't work for you. What works for someone else won't necessarily work for you. Because you are unique, you have to find your own way to trust that inner knowing about what is right for you and what you need to do.

Staying the course of positive change over the long haul requires persistence. You have to stick with it—even when the going gets tough. When it is slippery and you have poor traction, it's sometimes best to move forward slowly and maintain momentum rather than coming to a standstill. It also requires patience. You may have to wait out a storm or two before you can get moving again or see where you need to go. Staying the course requires the positive attitude that says, "I can do this!" Step after step, you focus on what's possible, what is working, how you have changed already and the strengths you can count on to move you towards what you want.

Resourceful Habits

Habits are something that you do automatically. While you may have started a particular habit through conscious effort (like brushing your teeth after meals), over time it has become established in your unconscious mind and you now do it regularly without having to think about it. It's important to note that not all habits are useful. You may, for instance, have had a habit of procrastinating or of eating sweets every evening. A resourceful habit could be to regularly apply some of the *Keys* you're learning in this book. This kind of habit will give you the consistency you need to make positive change. The key to long-term consistency is making it an automatic habit. That way, your unconscious mind takes over and you will do it regularly without having to think too much about it.

To get a new habit established, you'll need to use your conscious mind to remember to do it each day until it becomes automatic. The length of time to establish a habit varies with the complexity of what you are trying to establish, with your personality and with how motivated you are (you won't be able to establish a habit that you don't care about), but usually it takes about two months of regular practice.

It helps to do the activity at the same time each day and to link it into another practice: like doing a series of exercises or meditating before breakfast (eating seems to be something most people remember!) or journaling before bedtime. You can keep track of your progress by marking it on a calendar each day after you complete it. Reward yourself: even a simple acknowledgement of your victories can reinforce the behavior you are trying to establish. What habits do you want to set in place to help you create the changes you want in your life? What's in your unconscious mind will always override your conscious intentions. If you are trying to establish a resourceful habit but your unconscious is not in agreement with it, you will not be able to keep it going beyond how long you can use your willpower, which isn't usually very long!

Your unconscious mind takes your conscious thoughts as directions and it always finds the easiest way to do something. If you don't feel motivated and it's not urgent, what you are trying to get done will take a back burner to something you feel more strongly about. If you are trying to establish a habit about something you don't actually value, you will find it hard to gather the motivation to keep at it.

The Gift of Pain

I don't know about you, but I've had some clonks over the head when I needed to make change and wasn't doing it. When you are comfortable and doing well and you don't have a pressing problem, there is very little impetus for you to change. Opportunities for change come especially when the going gets rough and you feel uncomfortable. That's when you really want something to change and you are willing to put in the effort; it's often a useful time to hang in there and stick with it. The hard part is that even though the pain makes it an ideal time to change, most people habitually and unconsciously run back into old familiar places that feel safe. The result is that you end up staying stuck…and in pain.

Humans have a strong bias towards underestimating the harm of a bad habit (oh, just one more cookie won't hurt) and over estimating the benefits of a good one (I don't need to exercise today, I can do it tomorrow). How can you stay with practices you know are helpful when you aren't in pain? What's the best way for *you* to keep your exercise or mediation routine going? When you acknowledge your feelings of discomfort and uncertainty (your pain) and take it as an opportunity rather than a threat, you grow through the process and you will be more able to handle it next time it arises. You'll also have a lot of useful learning under your belt.

Dealing with Adversity and Setbacks

Each person deals with adversity and setbacks in a unique way. How do you do it? Do you step up to the challenge or do you think you've failed and shrink back? It's useful to know ahead of time how you tend to deal with challenges and decide how you want to deal with them this time. How will you keep your focus on what you want? The sooner you get back on track after a setback, the easier it will be to get going again. If you think of failures as important learning and feedback, which they are, they become a crucial part of your success. If you think of setbacks as failure, it's harder to make change.

When you feel stuck or have had a setback, remember that your unconscious mind takes direction from your conscious mind. Asking yourself open-ended questions is a powerful way to give direction to your unconscious mind. Keep asking, "How can I…?" "What should I do next?" "Where can I find…?" and let your unconscious mind present you with answers. The answers will come and they often pop up when you least expect it, like in the shower. Write them down as soon as you dry off (or keep some waterproof paper in the shower if that's where your inspiration arises!) and take action on them.

Flexibility

Flexibility is an essential quality in making positive change. If, like me, you tend to think you know the best and right way, it takes practice to be flexible and open to what comes forward and to make the best of it. You have many positive qualities and strengths; be flexible enough to bring forward the most useful one in any given situation. Sometimes it works best to use your logical rational mind; at other times your intuition will provide better guidance. Sometimes you need to be strong and firm and at other times gentle and yielding.

It takes practice to be flexible and open-minded—and it is a choice. You can decide to go with the flow of whatever happens when you focus on what you want. Follow your vision and choose growth and evolution over staying the same old course. Ask yourself which choice will help you to grow, do or become something different. Move towards choices that stretch you, that are outside of your comfort zone, and that move you into the unknown. Find your courage and have faith that if you focus on what you want, life will work in that direction.

Ninth Key: Things to Try

1. Think and write about a time that you stuck to something you really wanted to do. Why did you persist? How did you stay on track? What were the rewards?

2. Consider a problem you are having initiating or sticking to what you want to do. Do you truly value what it is you are trying to do? Does it matter strongly to you? Is there something else you would rather do?

3. Service to others is a cornerstone of all spiritual traditions, for good reason. It feels good and brings good things to you. When you help enough people with their problems; you find that your own problems go away. If you are struggling with your own pain, try offering your help to someone else.

The Tenth Key:
Find Supports Inside and Out

"Surround yourself with people who provide you with support and love and remember to give back as much as you can in return." Karen Kain

My independent streak showed up at a young age. According to my mom, who was trying to dress me at the time, my first words were "I do!" as I pushed her away and struggled to put on my clothes by myself. Like you might, I have pictures of me in a highchair with food all over my face (in fact, I had the bowl on my head!) as I practiced feeding myself. Not only are some of us born with a particular desire to do it ourselves, most people in the Western world are taught to value independence and figuring things out by ourselves, over interdependence and working in groups of support. There's a lot of encouragement for keeping your chin up, being strong and pretending everything is fine, even when it isn't. Independence can be a very useful quality; it can also keep you from gathering the support you need.

I can have a hard time sharing how I am feeling and what is going on with me, especially in times when I think I've made a mistake, something isn't good enough or I think someone is disappointed in me. It can feel vulnerable, uncomfortable and unsafe to admit that things aren't going as you expected or to admit your doubts and failures. Yet being vulnerable and admitting when things are not going so well is exactly what gives others the invitation and space to provide empathy, guidance and support. By learning how to be more upfront about my feelings and by sharing failures with others, I have been able to ask for the support I need. When you ask for support, you provide a model that can give other people permission to be vulnerable and to know that their mistakes are okay.

Do you have the support you need? What are your patterns of independence? When do they serve you well and when do they get in the way of getting the support you need?

The Motion of Emotions

There is a great transformative power in noticing and acknowledging what you are feeling. You might find it useful to think of emotions as red flags that are waving in various intensities to try to get your attention. They have an intelligence to share and will keep waving until you check in with them, acknowledge them and learn what you need to learn. Then they can go.

When you feel negative emotions about something that's happening, try noticing what you feel with compassion and curiosity. Own your feelings by speaking them out or writing about them. When you feel positive emotions, take the time to really experience and enjoy them as well. Taking the good stuff in will re-train your brain towards noticing what is positive in your life. It's also powerful after you acknowledge negative feelings or memories to bring to your mind a memory of a time when you felt happy and good about yourself. When you practice that pattern, the positive feeling gets linked to the negative one. When the negative one happens again, the positive one will be connected to it and will come to your mind as well. This is called "anchoring" in Neuro Linguistic Programming (NLP). Body energy tools like meridian tapping (EFT—Emotional Freedom Technique), where you state what's bothering you while you tap on a series of acupressure points, can also powerfully shift negative feelings and behaviors.

As much as it may seem that strong feelings hang in there, emotions continually shift. No one emotional state tends to last more than a minute or two. How you feel is your choice. You can choose to shift to emotions that serve you positively just as easily as staying in and reinforcing the ones that don't.

The human brain is wired for survival. As part of that imperative, you will notice and remember things that your unconscious mind identifies as potentially dangerous or threatening (negative things) much more than you will notice and remember the positive ones. It takes practice to train your brain to look for the best in others and in yourself. It helps to have people who focus on the positive around you and it helps to make a habit of actively planting positive key sentences about yourself in your mind as a kind of mantra ("I can do this!").

Positive comments and feedback and the attention you place on them need to strongly outnumber criticism in order for you to hear the positive and negative accurately and to respond to what you've heard in useful ways. You need to be connected to people who will give you positive feedback and help you to reflect back your strengths and successes. You also need some people who are willing to point out what's not always easy to see in yourself—your weaknesses and failings—and to help you learn from them. Praise and acknowledge the good and the successes in others and allow others to give that to you.

Modeling

This kind of modeling is not about strutting your stuff on the fashion runway (way out of my league unless it's a camping fashion show!). I'm talking about the powerful support that comes from copying someone who has already successfully done what you want to do. Find out how they think, act, and behave and how they motivate themselves and persist. Learn about how they get creative ideas and make good decisions, how they create self-discipline and see connections between things. Find out how they did what they wanted to do and model them—adopt the parts of their journey that will help you.

Try surrounding yourself with people who are successful in making positive change, who have travelled the road ahead of you and inspire you. It is supportive to have people in your life with which you can share your feelings, dreams and aspirations. The power of a group is much stronger than the power of an individual, so search out like-minded people to share ideas and work with collaboratively. Attend events with those who are doing what you want to do. Listen to motivational speakers, watch videos and read books on the topic. Find a mentor, advisor, teacher, or coach or get together a group of people who can support each other in moving towards what they want. Feed your mind what you want it to focus on in every way you can.

Not everyone will support your positive changes. When you start to do something positive about your problems and make changes in your life, people who are not ready to take action on their own problems may feel threatened and discourage your change. Are there people in your life that seem like friends but who argue for you to stay the same, encourage you to fear the unknown and to worry about risks? What about the people who focus on the negative and what's not working, or people who like to gossip about the failings and weaknesses of others? Do you want them in your life?

When do you do these things? The false supports inside and outside of you help you make excuses for why you shouldn't bother taking action to reach your goals. When you root these behaviors out of yourself and limit the time you spend with those kinds of people in your life, your overall experience will become more positive. Cut off the energy you waste on these unsupportive internal stories and external relationships. You may choose to end them or, if they are important to you for other reasons, be up front with those people. Tell them what kind of support you do want.

The wisdom of the body is another great source of guidance and support. Unlike the conscious mind and the ego, the body is very up front and it says it like it is. Like the unconscious mind, the body speaks in symbol and metaphor. What does it mean when people say things like, "I'm carrying the weight of the world on my shoulders?" or "He's a pain in the neck?" People intuitively know that what happens in the mind is related to the body, even when the connection is hard to understand. You may have a "gut feeling" about what is right and what is wrong for you.

When something feels right in your body, have you noticed that it turns out all right? When you ignore a feeling that you should or shouldn't do something, do you come to regret that you didn't listen? You may find that when you tune in to your body's signals you will feel lighter when something is right for you and heavy or dull when something is not right for you. Listen to your intuition—it's usually right.

Just as you would use discrimination about what you feed your body if you want it to be healthy, discriminate about what you feed your mind. Choose high quality, fresh and inspiring mind food for yourself. Give the message to your unconscious mind that you want to find positive and inspiring sources of books, discussions, and media. Make choices to eliminate the junk you may have been feeding your mind— sources that focus on violence, materialism, negativity and fear, for instance. Limit how much time you spend on your computer and jumping to notifications on your phone or other devices.

This final *Key* is about finding the supports inside and out that help you to focus on what you want in your life. It takes a shift in thinking to learn to trust that what happens to you is *your* creation, that the universe will support your evolution and that everything that happens to you is an opportunity to grow and learn what you came here to learn. Feeling and expressing gratitude for all the support you do have in your life will train your brain to notice and encourages more of it to come.

Tenth Key: Things to Try

1. Have a written conversation or dialogue with a trusted source of guidance, an aspect of the Divine, your Higher Self, or anything else that inspires and guides you. Find a quiet and private place where you can relax, get into your heart, and start a conversation on paper (or record it as you speak it out), as if you were writing a play in two parts. Say anything you wish and ask whatever you want to know and record your part and the response. Trust what comes in this form of channeling.

2. Take a "fast" from the news and media for a week and notice any difference in how you think and feel about yourself and the world as well as what you accomplish.

3. Try deleting the people from your contact lists that are dragging you down and wanting you to stay the same. Start looking for the kinds of people who will support and encourage what you want in your life.

The Wrap Up

Let's face it; life in a human body has its ups and downs. It ain't always easy to be human. The upside is that life in a human body has its fair share of pleasure and delight and it is a tremendous opportunity and privilege to grow and transform. Some would say that being human is the only way that we can evolve consciousness and reach enlightenment.

Regardless of whether your aim is to reach enlightenment or to make your life more meaningful and happy, making positive changes in your mind and life is certainly worth the effort.

You've been reading about some important principles of change in this book. Here's a quick overview of the *Ten Keys* to refresh your memory:

1. Open to Your Curiosity

- Cultivate your interest in who you are and what makes you tick; be curious about yourself

- Understand the roots of fear (genetic and learned) and choose to move past these limitations

- Be patient in waiting for the right doors to open, be courageous about leaving things behind that no longer fit you

- Be open to making mistakes and learning from them

- Remember that no matter what you've done or experienced, it's all part of being human. Give yourself a break.

- Don't hide in shame; share your experiences with others.

2. Know That Anything is Possible

- Invite infinite possibility through being in your heart, setting an intention and letting go of expectation

- Pay attention to what is different, not what is the same

- Notice the discomfort of uncertainty and stay there

- Watch for projection —own your stuff

- Remember that you don't have to change everything. Start with the most important and other things will fall away

3. Find Your Purpose and Passion

- Purpose is your calling

- Passion is what you love

- Follow your passion and doors will open

- Live in your genius, do what you love, love what you do

4. Use Your Mind and Beyond

- Use the focus of your conscious mind to direct your unconscious mind

- Connect with Source through your focus

- Focus on what you want

5. Get to the Heart of the Matter

- Remember the intelligence of your heart

- Balance your head with your heart

- Connect with Source through your heart

6. Discover What You Really Want

- Find out what you want versus what you think you should want

- Figure out what you value and believe

- Clear limiting beliefs

- Watch for upper limits and don't let them hold you down: consciously move past them

7. Focus on What You Want

- Know that you generate what is happening in your life

- Notice your focus, shift it to what you want

- Use your focus to direct the tremendous power of your unconscious mind

- Keep in mind that the human survival imperative drives you to stay safe and small. You don't have to stay there!

- Train yourself to pay attention to what is good and take the time to bring that in to yourself

8. Put What You Want into Action

- Envision what you want

- Set SMART goals —specific, measurable, attainable, realistic, timely

- Implement by taking the best step you can think of and trying it out

- Seek and learn from feedback

- Evaluate how it is going and take your next action

9. **Stay the Course**

- Your life experiences give you traction
- Persistence pays off, keep going!
- Cultivate resourceful habits
- Pain is a motivating force for change
- Know how you will deal with adversity and setbacks
- Be flexible

10. **Find Supports Inside and Out**

- Recognize your tendencies towards independence
- Seek the support you need
- Use the intelligence of your emotions to direct you
- Seek and accept positive feedback and use criticism wisely
- Model after someone who has gone before you

Do you want to make lasting positive change in your life?

- Sign up for the free monthly *Guiding Positive Change Newsletter* at www.guidingpositivechange.com and check out blog articles of interest

- Try the personal coaching, healing packages, workshops and classes of Sohlea Rico of Guiding Positive Change

- You can Skype, use Google Hangouts, or phone from anywhere in the world or come in person to Courtenay, BC, Canada

- Experience rapid and lasting transformation in thinking, behaviors, feelings and physical wellbeing

- The approach is tailored to your unique needs and personality

- Get one on one attention from a relaxed and highly skilled practitioner

- I specialize in working with middle-aged women and my work is suitable for other adults

- Do you wonder if working with *Guiding Positive Change* will be a good fit for you? Contact Sohlea Rico at info@guidingpositivechange.com to arrange a *free fifteen minute consultation* by Skype or phone

Made in the USA
San Bernardino, CA
11 October 2014